Eternal Reverberations

The Echoes Within

A Book of Poems (2008-2023)

Aditya Vesh Pandey

ISBN 979-8-89233-747-2

Dedication

To Dear Papa, Maa and my brother Avani...

Thanks for loads of things. Without you I am nothing...

Dedication

To Dear Papa, Maa and my brother Avani...

Thanks for loads of things. Without you I am nothing...

Contents

BharatVarsh – Oldest Continuously Surviving Civilization

Historical Legends of Bharat

Comprehending Comprehensions

Prologue

Welcome to the world of poetry, where words dance on the fine line between logic and magic, creating a space that allows you to explore the mystical while still anchoring in the rational.

Poetry, for me, has always been a refuge—a language that transcends the limitations of mere logic. As a child, I found solace in the verses that effortlessly expressed the nuances of life, going beyond the confines of straightforward prose.

My poetic journey took flight when I entered the realm of the IT corporate world, my struggle in navigating the bustling metropolitan cities and the solitude that came with it. Amid the corporate hustle, I discovered poetry as my escape—a means to form my own team with myself when the conventional paths didn't resonate with my spirit.

Traversing through various landscapes, both physical and emotional, I delved into the rich tapestry of folklores and histories shared by my parents and grand parents. Fuelling my curiosity, I embarked on a personal quest to validate these tales & legends through my own experiences.

Acknowledging the unique perceptions each one of us holds, I began meeting diverse souls, visiting new places, and documenting my observations. This amalgamation of personal encounters and reflections finds its expression in my poems. Whether it's capturing the essence of my observations about sacred spaces , places I have visited or folks I have met, the rhythmic hum of cosmos, Ancient Indian civilization, various contemporary events etc. my verses mirror the kaleidoscope of my experiences about this only oldest continuously surviving great civilization called Indic Civilization.

From the intricacies of yoga to contemplations on the creation of the cosmos, my poetry spans the spectrum. It delves into the microscopic world of Atoms to Cosmic world of Black holes , pays homage to historical figures like Sapta Rishis, Shri Ram chandra ji, Aryabhatta, and explores the sacredness of places like Kailash – the king of mountains, Kashi & Shri Ayodhya ji etc.

The poems within this collection are the echoes of my heart. I hope they resonate with you, connecting your heartbeat to the rhythm of divine. Wishing you a delightful sojourn through the realms of words and emotions.

With love and devotion,

Aadi

शिव चला

घनी धूप से छाँवों से,
और कंदराओं गुफाओं से,
हिमालय से इंदु तलक,
हैं कई हृदय पर एक धड़क,
एक ही जीवन, एक ही झलक,
शिव चला शिव चला ।

महा विनाशक, देवों के देव,
जय जय शंकर महादेव।
माता पिता के आशीषों से,
गुरुओं की शिक्षा दीक्षा से,
और सभ्यता की प्रत्यांचा पर,
यह अस्त्र बना ब्रह्मास्त्र बना,
शिव चला शिव चला ।

ढोल ताश नगाड़ों पर,
और नदियों पर और तालों पर,
शंख नाद की अघोर ध्वनि,
उसपर स्पंदित होती है अवनि,
उस रश्मि रथी की आभा को समेट,
शिव चला शिव चला ।

नाद ही ब्रह्मा विश्व स्वरूपा,
अडिग अमर और निर्भय रूपा,
उन्माद भरा संस्कार में पिरो कर,
जीव पनप रहा स्नेह से भिगोकर,
आस लिए, सीखने की प्यास लिए,
शिव चला शिव चला ।

काल चक्र ब्रह्म नाद का हिस्सा,
समझ रहा ये कैसा किस्सा,
अदभुत निराला ये करता शोर,
इसने थामी है स्वयं की डोर,
स्वयं ही करता स्वयं की भोर,
शिव चला शिव चला ।

अलंकार के संस्मरण में,
प्रकृति के जीवन और मरण में,
आच्छादित होती ओंकार की वाणी,
कह गए ज्ञानी और बलिदानी,
है क्यों भारत भूमि जानी मानी,
और ना जानो तो क्या है हानि,
इसी खोज में समाहित पड़ा,
शिव चला शिव चला ।

चुनौतियों से घिरा पड़ा,
मूल में निःशब्द स्थिर खड़ा,
कर्म से ये खेल रहा,

नित्य नियम से दंड पेल रहा,
साधना से और उपासना से,
मनोकामना और धारणा से,
सब में लीन, पर जागृत सब देख रहा,
शिव चला शिव चला ।

 आदि

Creation and Mysticism

Rudra – The Roarer

In the cosmic dance, a Roarer's might,
Lord Rudra – The Roarer, in the eternal night.
The echo of a series, a cosmic rhyme,
Big bangs resound, transcending time.

Eighty-four universes, a mystical score,
In each, a trace of the ones before.
Subtle whispers, echoes divine,
In the cosmic fabric, where stars align.

Rudra, the Roarer, in Vedic lore,
The roaring sound, creation's core.
Eradicator of problems, at their root,
In the cosmic symphony, a resolute pursuit.

Shiva Sahasranama, the sacred chant,
Rudra's name, in devotion, enchant.
The Shri Rudram hymn, an ancient plea,
Dedicated to Rudra, in cosmic glee.

In Namakam's verses, the primal call,
Sadasiva, the mighty, the Lord of all.
Mahadeva, in divine embrace,
In the vast cosmos, a sacred space.

String theory's dance, a cosmic play,
Rudra's Roar, in every array.
Confirmation in ancient insight,
Science and mysticism, a union bright.

Sound, the essence, creation's hymn,
Rudra's Roar, the cosmic vim.
Big Bang's echo, through time and space,
In Rudra's roar, all find their place.

Aadi

AUMKAR – The Ultimate Reverberation

In the cosmic symphony, a sacred hum,
Resonates the essence, the eternal Aum.
From galaxies to atoms, in every space,
A sound that holds the universe in embrace.

AUM, the primordial, the cosmic chant,
In every particle, in every plant.
A frequency that science begins to trace,
NASA, ISRO, CERN unveil its grace.

In the vastness of space, where galaxies twirl,
AUM echoes, in the cosmic swirl.
NASA's telescopes, eyes to the sky,
Capture vibrations, as AUM passes by.

Waves of sound, through the cosmic sea,
ISRO's satellites, witness the AUM's decree.
Radiating from stars, in celestial trance,
AUM's frequencies in a cosmic dance.

CERN's colliders, in the pursuit of the small,
Reveal the secrets, in particle's call.
AUM, the resonance in the tiniest trace,
In the fabric of reality, in every space.

Planets, moons, and stars align,
AUM's vibrations, in every design.
A cosmic choir, a universal hymn,
AUM's frequencies, through dimensions swim.

In quantum realms, where mysteries unfold,
AUM's presence, in particles untold.
The strings of existence, vibrating in tune,
AUM's melody, in the cosmic monsoon.

Galaxies hum, planets sing,
AUM's resonance, creation's spring.
Scientific reports, facts unfold,
AUM, the frequency, in the cosmic gold.

From the macro to the micro, in cosmic ballet,
AUM's vibrations, in every array.
The fabric of spacetime, in its embrace,
AUM contains all, in its sacred grace.

In the labs of knowledge, where scientists peer,
AUM's frequencies, crystal clear.
The universe sings, in a cosmic rhyme,
AUM, the pulse of space and time.

So in the quiet moments, when silence calls,
Listen closely, as the cosmic AUM enthralls.
In the vastness of space, in the smallest particle's plume,
AUM reverberates, in the cosmic womb.

 Aadi

Shivoham

In the stillness of the cosmic night,
Lord Shiva, a being of profound might.
With ash-covered skin, and a third eye's sight,
He's the embodiment of truth and light.

A crescent moon adorns his tangled hair,
A river of Ganga, he gracefully bears.
Nandi, his bull, ever loyal and fair,
In his divine presence, we all find solace there.

He's the Lord of dance, Nataraja's name,
With cosmic rhythm, the universe he tames.
His dance of destruction, a celestial flame,
To create a new, he plays the cosmic game.

In deep meditation, on Mount Kailash's peak,
He withdraws from the world, in solitude he seeks.
Yet, he's a father, a husband, a sage so meek,
Lord Shiva, the mystic, the essence of the unique.

In the sacred waters of the Ganges' flow,
Devotees find salvation, letting their sins go.
With a serpent coiled around his neck, we know,
Lord Shiva's blessings, a divine, eternal show.

As the Lord of transformation and rebirth,
Shiva's presence is felt all over the Earth.
In his devotion, we find boundless worth,
For he's the destroyer and creator of our birth.

Aadi

Play Of Five Elements

In the cosmic tapestry, where creation weaves,
The five elements, the dance of cosmic leaves.
Earth, water, fire, air, and ether's embrace,
A symphony of elements, in the cosmic space.

Vedas' verses, ancient and grand,
Speak of the elements, in cosmic command.
Upanishads whisper in timeless hymns,
The dance of elements, where creation begins.

Earth, the stable foundation beneath,
Where life takes root, in the cosmic sheath.
From Vedas' hymns to Puranas' lore,
Earth, the cradle where existence explores.

Water, the fluid essence in flow,
Life's elixir, in rivers that grow.
From Upanishads' verses to timeless tales,
Water's wisdom, in ancient trails.

Fire, the radiant energy's dance,
Transforming matter, in a cosmic trance.
In the Puranas' flames and Vedas' pyres,
Fire's essence, where creation aspires.

Air, the breath of life's gentle sigh,
In the cosmic breeze, where mysteries lie.
From ancient scriptures to cosmic winds,
Air's whispers, where creation begins.

Ether, the boundless cosmic expanse,
Where stars align, in the cosmic dance.
In Upanishads' silence and Vedas' hymns,
Ether's presence, where creation swims.

In Shiva's discourse, the elements profound,
A yogic journey, where truths are found.
The Pancha Bhutas, in Shiva's embrace,
In the cosmic dance, where elements trace.

Shiva, the master of cosmic ballet,
In the five elements, his presence lay.
The Sapta Rishis, in sacred trance,
Received the science, the yogic advance.

Seven sages, in devotion's flame,
Learned the secrets, from Shiva they came.
The dance of elements, a cosmic scroll,
In the yogic science, Shiva's role.

So in the cosmic ballet, where elements play,
Shiva's wisdom, in the ancient array.
From the Pancha Bhutas to the yogic trance,
Elements and Shiva, in the cosmic dance.

 Aadi

Cosmic Dance of Natraj

In the cosmic theatre, where galaxies twirl,
Behold the cosmic dance of Natraj, a celestial swirl.
Particles pirouette in the vast cosmic space,
In the grand ballet of creation, a rhythmic embrace.

Nataraja, the cosmic dancer, with cosmic might,
Whirls through dimensions in the eternal night.
With Shiva's cosmic energy, a dance divine,
A cosmic spectacle, where universes entwine.

In the quantum waltz, particles unite,
Balletic motions, in the cosmic light.
Neutrinos and quarks in a mesmerizing trance,
In the cosmic dance, a harmonious advance.

Galaxies spin like dancers on a cosmic stage,
Nataraja's presence, in every cosmic page.
Black holes and stars in a cosmic trance,
A dance of creation, in the cosmic expanse.

Strings of energy in a rhythmic sway,
Cosmic dance of Natraj, in the Milky Way.
Gravitational waves in a cosmic romance,
A prance of forces, in the cosmic dance.

In the cosmic ballet, where time and space entwine,
Natraj's dance, a cosmic design.
In the cosmic theatre, where wonders enhance,
Natraj's cosmic dance, invites us to Shiva's lap to entrance.

 Aadi

Nandi – An Eternal Active Waiting

Nandi, the devoted bull, strong and grand,
In the sacred land, he takes his stand.
Guardian of Shiva, in the temple sand,
A symbol of loyalty, forever in demand.

With eyes of wisdom, a tranquil soul,
Beside Lord Shiva, his presence whole.
In devotion, he plays a vital role,
As the divine bond between heart and goal.

A silent witness to the cosmic dance,
In Shiva's abode, he's given a chance.
With strength and grace, a mystical trance,
Nandi's presence, a divine romance.

In every temple, his statue we see,
A symbol of faith and humility.
Nandi, the bull, in devotion's decree,
Guiding our spirits to eternity.

Aadi

String Theory

In the cosmic tapestry, where realms entwine,
A mystic dance, a theory divine.
Threads of existence, unseen and untold,
A symphony of strings, mysteries unfold.

In the fabric of space, where dimensions weave,
Strings vibrating, a cosmic spell they conceive.
Harmonies resonate in the celestial expanse,
A cosmic ballet, where particles dance.

Microcosmic whispers, vibrations so small,
Yet in their dance, universes enthral.
A cosmic orchestra, strings humming a tune,
Echoes of creation in the vast cosmic dune.

In the labyrinth of theories, where time bends,
Strings intertwine, reality transcends.
A cosmic web, woven with threads unseen,
In the cosmic loom, where wonders convene.

Dimensions ripple, like waves in the night,
String theory unfolds, a celestial light.
A dance of energy, in the cosmic ballet,
Strings of creation, in the vast astral play.

In the tapestry of existence, where secrets unfurl,
Strings of destiny, in the cosmic swirl.
A mystical realm, where reality's spun,
In the enchanting dance of strings, a cosmic union.

 Aadi

Black Holes

In the cosmic tapestry, where myths align,
Black holes emerge in the ancient design.
Scriptures speak of celestial beings and lore,
As dimensions dance around a cosmic core.

Lord Shiva, the cosmic dancer in the night,
Black holes echo in his mystical might.
A dance with gravity, a celestial embrace,
In the vastness of space, a sacred space.

A singularity, where gravity is profound,
A cosmic force where time is unbound.
The fabric of space bends, a mystical rhyme,
As black holes carve through the cosmic grime.

In ancient tales, beings traverse the void,
Dimensions entwined, in existence coiled.
Black holes as portals, a cosmic gate,
Where time and space intimately relate.

Gravity's grip, an unyielding force,
Black holes bend it, changing the course.
A celestial whirlpool, where light may drown,
In the cosmic ocean, where mysteries abound.

In the heart of darkness, where light disappears,
Black holes whisper in cosmic spheres.
A mystic veil, where dimensions blend,
In the cosmic dance, where stories transcend.

Lord Shiva, the cosmic dancer's embrace,
Black holes mirror his mystical grace.
In the stillness of meditation, where realms combine,
A dance with the infinite, where mysteries entwine.

A singularity, a point of no return,
Where the laws of physics cease to discern.
In the cosmic ballet, where wonders unfold,
Black holes, portals to a universe untold.

In the ancient scriptures, a cosmic thread,
Black holes hinted, where the mystics tread.
Beings from dimensions, a cosmic stroll,
In the gravitational dance, where black holes enroll.

Through the cosmic whirlpool, where time takes a bend,
In the embrace of black holes, mysteries blend.
Lord Shiva, the cosmic dancer in the night,
Black holes echo in his mystical light.

 Aadi

Atomic to Cosmic

In the tapestry of atoms, a cosmic rhyme,
Tiny dancers, electrons in their prime.
Orbiting the nucleus, a celestial ballet,
In the microcosm, where forces sway.

Ancient scriptures hint at cosmic kin,
Atoms and universe, akin.
Vedic echoes in the cosmic verse,
Atoms dance, the universe rehearse.

Atoms, galaxies in a grand design,
In the cosmic dance, a common sign.
Electrons spin, like stars in the night,
In the vast expanse of cosmic light.

The universe whispers in atomic codes,
Atoms echo in the cosmic abodes.
Similarities resonate in the dance,
Atoms and galaxies, a shared expanse.

Lord Shiva, the cosmic dancer's embrace,
In atoms' dance, a mystical grace.
Nataraja, the Lord of the Cosmic Ring,
In every particle, his presence sings.

In the dance of electrons, a sacred twist,
Particles in motion, in Shiva's tryst.
The nucleus, a lingam in the core,
Lord Shiva's dance, forevermore.

Shiva's cosmic dance, an eternal play,
In atoms' dance, in every array.
The dance of particles, a divine trance,
Lord Shiva's cosmic, subatomic dance.

In the vast cosmic sea, atoms swim,
Galaxies twirl in a celestial hymn.
Atoms and universe, intertwined,
In Lord Shiva's dance, secrets bind.

So in the quantum realm and cosmic night,
Atoms and galaxies, a shared light.
In Lord Shiva's dance, a cosmic tie,
A mystical union, where realities lie.

Aadi

Sacred Spaces

Mount Kailash – The Abode of Lord Shiva

In the realm where heavens and earth entwine,
Holy Mount Kailash, where divine spirits shine.
Nestled in Tibet's embrace, a sacred abode,
A mountain of legends, where gods bestowed.

Beneath the shadow of Kailash's height,
Lake Manasarovar and Rakshastal unite.
The Indus, Sutlej, Brahmaputra's stream,
In reverence to Kailash, their origins deem.

Upon the ancient rocks, a geological tale,
Faults and folds in the Himalayan scale.
Metasedimentary pendant, granite base,
Nature's hand in Mount Kailash's grace.

Sacred in Hindu, Jain, and Buddhist lore,
A pilgrimage destination forevermore.
Shiva's abode, a divine residence,
With Parvati, Ganesha, and Kartikeya's presence.

In Ramayana's tale, Ravana's bold quest,
To uproot Kailash, a futile test.
Shiva's toe, a mountain's embrace,
Ravananugraha, a symbol of grace.

Mahabharata's epic journey told,
Pandavas climb, in search to go beyond.
Gateway to heavens, Svarga's door,
Mount Kailash, where the devas adore.

Vishnu Purana's crystal facets unfold,
Ruby, gold, lapis lazuli, stories told.
A lotus pillar at creation's heart,
A realm where mystic realms depart.

In Jainism, Ashtapada's sacred ground,
Rishabhadeva's nirvana found.
Emperor Bharata's shrines so divine,
On Kailash's heights, a Jain design.

Buddhist texts name it Meru's peak,
Cakrasaṃvara's bliss, Buddhists seek.
Padmasambhava's presence graced,
In Kailash's mystic spaces embraced.

Milarepa's challenge, a sorcerer's flight,
Battling Bönchung, a mystical sight.
Kailash, witness to enlightenment's quest,
A sacred mountain, where faith finds rest.

 Aadi

Shri Amarnath

In the cradle of Himalayas, where glaciers gleam,
Amarnath, a shrine, a celestial dream.
At an altitude high, where the heavens kiss,
A sacred journey, a pilgrimage of bliss.

Through Sind Valley's embrace, a pilgrimage grand,
Snowy peaks and glaciers, a divine land.
In Pahalgam or Sonamarg, the journey starts,
To the abode of Shiva, where devotion imparts.

A cave at 3,888 meters, a sacred abode,
A shrine revered, where pilgrims are bestowed.
Amidst snow and ice, a mystical story unfolds,
The Amarnath Yatra, where spirituality moulds.

Mahamaya Shakti Pitha, an energy divine,
One of the fifty-one, where sacred forces entwine.
Sati's fallen parts, in holy reverence held,
In the Amarnath cave, where devotion is spelled.

The Swayambhu lingam, a stalagmite's grace,
A natural formation, in the sacred space.
At 3,888 meters, where the mountains stand tall,
The lingam of Shiva, a divine call.

A solid dome, a stalagmite's art,
Formed by water's freeze, a spiritual part.
In the heart of the cave, where echoes resound,
The lingam, Parvati, and Ganesha, profound.

The Mahabharata whispers, the Puranas sing,
The lingam's tale, through eternity's spring.
From May to August, the wax and wane,
As Himalayan snow, a cosmic reign.

Believers hold, as the moon takes its flight,
The lingam grows, in the summer's light.
A secret shared, in divine revelation,
Where Shiva spoke of life, an eternal narration.

Lidder Valley cradles the cave's serenity,
Glaciers and secrets in nature's divinity.
Limestone and gypsum, the cave's embrace,
Heat of devotion, affecting the sacred space.

Amarnath, a pilgrimage of devotion and grace,
A journey to the sacred, a celestial embrace.
In the heart of the Himalayas, where echoes sing,
A mystical sojourn, to the divine spring.

 Aadi

Shri Kedarnath

In the Himalayan heights, where spirits soar,
Kedarnath Temple, a sacred door.
Nestled amidst peaks, a timeless shrine,
Divinity echoes in each prayer and sign.

At the confluence of rivers, a celestial blend,
The Mandakini's whispers, the Bhagirathi's descend.
In the lap of snow-clad peaks so high,
Kedarnath stands beneath the azure sky.

A sanctum of Shiva, the Lord of the peaks,
Where devotion speaks, the soul seeks.
Amidst the Kedar range, where echoes chime,
Kedarnath, a pilgrimage through space and time.

Adi Guru Shankaracharya, in reverence's trance,
Chose Kedarnath for his sacred dance.
A sage profound, in penance deep,
Within these realms, his vows did keep.

With the river's hymn and mountain's call,
Shankaracharya, in devotion's thrall.
In solitude's embrace, his soul did roam,
Beneath the peaks, he found his home.

Through icy winds and rugged trail,
Shankara's journey, determination's sail.
In Kedarnath's shadow, where echoes play,
He meditated, where gods held sway.
Glacial streams, in reverence, flow,
In the temple's presence, devotees bow.
From rocky trails to the temple's door,
A journey of faith, devotion's core.

The temple's spire, a beacon of the divine,
Kedarnath's aura, where gods entwine.
Amidst the rugged terrain, in solitude,
The temple stands, a symbol of fortitude.

In the Garhwal Himalayas, where sages trod,
Kedarnath, abode of the benevolent god.
Adorned by snow, in celestial embrace,
A sanctified haven, a sacred space.

Pilgrims ascend, in devotion's trance,
To Kedarnath's shrine, a sacred dance.
With every step, a prayer unfolds,
In the temple's sanctum, eternity moulds.

Kedarnath, where the heavens descend,
A sacred saga, where spirits mend.
In the echoes of chants and temple bells,
Divine serenity within Kedarnath dwells.

 Aadi

Kashi – The City of Eternal Light

In the tapestry of time, where history weaves,
Varanasi stands, where the Ganges receives.
Kashi, the ancient name whispered by sages,
A city that echoes through timeless pages.

In Sarnath's shadow, a lion's grace,
A symbol of Buddha's inaugural embrace.
Varanasi's soil, where sermons were spun,
The eternal city, a tale begun.

Eighth-century echoes, Adi Shankara's feat,
Establishing Shiva's worship, a sacred seat.
Varanasi's ghats, a spiritual shore,
Where devotion's flames forever soar.

Varanasi, a city of the learned and wise,
Philosophers, poets, under Ganga's skies.
Musical notes, in the Benares breeze,
A city where art and wisdom tease.

Tulsidas' pen, on Kashi's ground,
In Awadhi verses, the Ramayana rewound.
Bhakti's heartbeat in every line,
A city where divine stories entwine.

Kabir and Ravidas, born in its embrace,
Bhakti's essence, a sacred grace.
In Varanasi's heart, devotion's swell,
A city where saints and poets dwell.

Varanasi, a city of the learned and wise,
Philosophers, poets, under Ganga's skies.
Musical notes, in the Benares breeze,
A city where art and wisdom tease.

Sanskrit's cradle, Benares Sanskrit College's birth,
In the East India Company's rule, a scholarly hearth.
Nationalism's dawn, in education's name,
Madan Mohan Malviya's vision, the spark of a flame.

Central Hindu College, in 1898's light,
A torchbearer in education's flight.
Banaras Hindu University, a modern ode,
A legacy on Kashi's ancient road.

Varanasi, a city of the learned and wise,
Philosophers, poets, under Ganga's skies.
Musical notes, in the Benares breeze,
A city where art and wisdom tease.

Kashi, the City of Light's eternal glow,
Epithets in Sanskrit, a sacred flow.
Avimukta, never forsaken by Shiva's hand,
In the luminous city, where gods stand.

Rudravāsa, where Rudra finds repose,
Mahāshmashāna, where life's river slows.
Varanasi, in epithets adorned,
A city, where the birth and death both are deeply celebrated & mourned.

In Varanasi's alleys, where echoes persist,
A city's heart, where time does exist.
Kashi, the eternal, in Ganga's embrace,
A tapestry woven in divine grace.

Aadi

Shri Ayodhya Ji

In Ayodhya's soil, where legends tread,
A tapestry of significance, widely spread.
Beyond the archaeological whispers and lore,
Ayodhya's importance, resonates evermore.

For every Indian heart, Ayodhya's the core,
A cultural anchor, forever to adore.
No India without Ayodhya's grace,
In every citizen's soul, a sacred place.

Shri Ram, the embodiment of noble might,
In Ayodhya's story, a guiding light.
A symbol of dharma, righteousness' flame,
Ayodhya's legacy, in every Indian's name.

Ram Rajya's dream, in Ayodhya's embrace,
A vision for India, a divine space.
To establish peace, balance, and grace,
Ayodhya's role, in the world's embrace.

No India without Ayodhya's call,
In every heart, resonates for all.
A cultural epicentre, a nation's pride,
Ayodhya's significance, far and wide.

To change the world order, a cosmic quest,
In Ayodhya's narrative, a divine bequest.
For harmony and peace to unfurl,
Ayodhya's importance, in every swirl.

In the saga of Rama, a timeless theme,
Ayodhya's relevance, a nation's dream.
To bring balance to the cosmic scale,
Ayodhya's tale, in every heart, prevails.

So, Ayodhya, a beacon bright,
Guiding India with eternal light.
A sacred space, a cultural anchor true,
Ayodhya's importance, in every view.

 Aadi

Mathura Vrindavan

In Mathura's sacred soil, where history breathes,
A tapestry of legends, where divinity weaves.
Vrindavan's embrace, where Krishna plays,
A spiritual haven in the sun's warm rays.

Mathura, the city where Krishna was born,
A celestial event on that auspicious morn.
The prison where Devaki and Vasudeva reside,
Yet, in Krishna's love, their hearts abide.

Vrindavan's groves, where the Gopis dance,
Radha and Krishna, in love's sweet trance.
The Raas Leela, a divine spectacle,
In Vrindavan's realm, where love does excel.

For every Indian heart, Mathura is the start,
A pilgrimage to the soul, a sacred part.
No India without Mathura's grace,
In every soul, a divine space.

In Mahabharata's verses, Mathura shines,
A city's tale in the epic's lines.
Krishna's alliance with the Pandava's plight,
Mathura's role, in the cosmic fight.

Dwaraka's kingdom, by the ocean's side,
A city of grandeur, in history's stride.
Mathura's connection, a celestial thread,
In Krishna's journey, where love is spread.

Shri Krishna's teachings on Kurukshetra's plain,
Guidance to Arjuna, in battle's strain.
Mathura's essence in wisdom's stream,
In every discourse, where truths beam.

To change every human from within,
In Mathura's embrace, where virtues begin.
To awaken the soul, a divine swirl,
Mathura's tale, in every heart, unfurl.

Vrindavan's dance, a mystical theme,
A celestial rhythm in every dream.
To bring peace and balance to the human heart,
Mathura – Vrindavan's grace, a timeless art.

So, Mathura – Vrindavan, a spiritual light,
Guiding India with divine insight.
A sacred space, a cultural anchor true,
Mathura – Vrindavan's importance, in every view.

 Aadi

Ujjaini – City of Mahakaal

In the heart of India, where history breathes,
Ujjain stands, where time enwreathes.
Avantika, Ujjaini, in ancient lore,
A city with tales, forevermore.

Maharaja Vikramaditya's rule,
In Ujjain's embrace, a kingdom cool.
A cradle of civilization, where legends thrive,
In the land where lore of Vikram and Betal survive.

Kalidas, the bard, in Ujjain born,
His verses like the morning dawn.
In the city's essence, poetic grace,
Ujjain's legacy, in time's embrace.

Vedas' whispers on Shipra's shore,
Ujjain's ancient tales, forevermore.
In scriptures, Puranas, and Upanishads' light,
Ujjain's heritage, in the cosmic sight.

Mahakaal, the King of Time,
In Ujjain's temple, in rhythm and rhyme.
A cradle of time, where legends unfurl,
In the Mahakaal's cosmic swirl.

Jantar Mantar, an ancient clock,
In Ujjain's soil, where time's ticks knock.
A city that once counted the world's pace,
In Ujjain's history, a timeless grace.

On Shipra's banks, the city stands,
Where ancient legends walk on sands.
Ujjain, the clock of time in yore,
A city where history and myths explore.

In Vikramaditya's reign, Ujjain's prime,
A kingdom where tales intertwine.
From Kalidas' verses to Mahakaal's chime,
Ujjain's saga, a timeless rhyme.

So in the heart of India, Ujjain's tale,
A city where legends set sail.
On Shipra's banks, where time was spun,
Ujjain, the ancient city, forever one.

 Aadi

Jai Shri Mahakaal – A Cosmic Ode

In the cosmic expanse where galaxies twirl,
MahaKaal, the eternal, unfurls.
Endless and timeless, like the radiant sun,
You are the essence of creation, where all is spun.

In your name, time's cycles repeat,
With every dawn and dusk, the universe you greet.
Gentle and discreet, a force of nature's own,
MahaKaal, in your presence, we find our throne.

The Tandava's grace in your cosmic dance,
Creation and destruction find their chance.
With each step, a new era takes its place,
In life's grand theatre, you hold all the space.

With ash-covered skin, Ganga in your locks,
Symbolizing purity that time never mocks.
In Kashi's embrace, your presence does glow,
MahaKaal, to your devotion, we humbly bow.

Nandi, the loyal guardian with might,
In the silent realm of day and night.
MahaKaal, in your cosmic light,
You guide our souls to infinite height.

In Shiva's heart, you eternally reside,
As MahaKaal, your power can't hide.
In your name, we seek truth far and wide,
In your boundless grace, our spirits confide.

Jai Shri Mahakaal, the timeless one,
In the cosmic symphony, where all is spun.
Guide us through the cycles, under the sun,
MahaKaal, in your name, our spirits are one.

In Ujjain's heart, where history unfolds,
MahaKaal's tale, in stone it's told.
Bhasma Aarti, a ritual so divine,
Where time and eternity entwine.

Ujjain, the city where Mahakaal reigns,
In history's embrace, where time remains.
A cradle ancient, with stories untold,
MahaKaal's mysteries, in temples unfold.

Through the ages, your presence persists,
In the sands of time, where history exists.
Mahakaal, the witness of every birth and demise,
In the river of time, where every moment lies.

Bhasma Aarti, where ash becomes art,
Symbol of life's transient, from end to start.
In Ujjain's dusk, under the celestial dome,
MahaKaal's presence finds its sacred home.

From the echoes of Sandipani's lore,
To the pulse of Ujjain, where pilgrims explore.
MahaKaal, in Ujjain's timeless trance,
A sanctuary where seekers find their chance.

In Ujjain's whispers, where MahaKaal's story's told,
Bhasma Aarti's flame, ancient and bold.
Jai Shri Mahakaal, in devotion we proclaim,
In the heart of Ujjain, MahaKaal's eternal flame.

 Aadi

Maa Rewa

In the sanctum of Amarkantak, where shadows unfold,
Maa Rewa, Narmada river, in mystic tales is told.
From the sacred soils of Vindhyachal's embrace,
Her journey begins, a river of divine grace.

Amarakantak, the cradle of her birth,
Narmada flows, a pilgrimage of worth.
Through Vindhya's arms, in a gentle hold,
A sacred narrative, an ancient story told.

Satpura, the silent sentinel she passes by,
Guardian peaks beneath the azure sky.
In their shadows, she weaves history's thread,
Narmada, a river where legends are bred.

Through the ancient lands, her waters weave,
A hymn of devotion, a journey to believe.
Temples and ghats along her sacred shore,
Narmada's currents, a timeless lore.

In the heart of India, she winds and turns,
A lifeline to cultures, where history discerns.
Through empires and kingdoms, a witness true,
Narmada river, in antiquity she grew.

Cities and shrines along her flow,
Whisper tales of devotion that continue to grow.
In the embrace of mountains, she shaped,
Ancient Indian history, in every bend draped.

Maa Rewa, with currents strong and pure,
In her journey, ancient history ensures.
A sacred river, through time she wends,
Narmada, where the ancient saga never ends.

 Aadi

BharatVarsh – Oldest Continuously Surviving Civilization

Bharat – God's Very Own Country

Bharat, a name that history weaves,
In the vast tapestry where every soul seeks.
From the Himalayan peaks to the ocean's crest,
A saga unfolds, where civilizations nest.

From the sacred Ganges to the Thar's golden sand,
In your diverse landscapes, a nation grand.
Mountains and rivers, deserts wide, Bharat,
in your embrace, stories reside.

In Rigveda's hymns, your rivers flow,
In Puranas' tales, your mountains glow.
From Ayodhya's plains to Dwarka's shore,
In mythic realms, your essence we adore.

Bharat, a symphony of cultures so vast,
In your unity, diverse voices cast.
From Kashmir's chill to Kanyakumari's balm,
In every heartbeat, you find your calm.

In Mahabharata's war, Kuru's fate entwined,
Ramayana's verses in Ayodhya's bind.
From Harappa's ruins to Ashoka's reign,
Bharat, in time's scroll, your stories gain.

In your soil, empires rise and fall,
A dance of dynasties, a historical call.
Mauryas, Guptas, Cholas, and more,
Bharat, each era leaves its lore.

In the pages of civics, a democratic flame,
From ancient councils to a modern acclaim.
Republics of yore to a sovereign stand,
Bharat, evolving with a democratic hand.

In Sabha and Samiti, where voices soared,
In Rajya and Lok Sabha, democracy restored.
From Ashoka's edicts to the Preamble's art,
Bharat, you govern with a democratic heart.

In your essence, resilience is found,
Through challenges faced, on sacred ground.
From the Mauryan pillars to the Parliament's dome,
Bharat, you've built a democratic home.

In Vedas' hymns and Upanishads' quest,
In folklore's whispers, your spirit's blessed.
In every ritual and festive cheer,
Bharat, your essence is crystal clear.

Diwali's lights and Holi's hues,
Navratri's beats and Eid's sweet cues.
Gurupurab's grace and Pongal's cheer,
Bharat, your festivals bring hearts near.

Bharat, in your name, a legacy we bear,
A nation's story, a collective prayer.
In your tapestry, every thread is rare,
Bharat, a journey beyond compare.

 Aadi

Sapta Sindhu – The Seven Sacred Rivers Of Bharat

In the sacred land of Bharat, where rivers weave,
Sapta Sindhu, the seven, in beauty conceive.
Indus, Ganges, Yamuna, Saraswati's grace,
A riverine symphony, in history's embrace.

Vedas' hymns, in ancient lore,
Sing of rivers that ancient seers adore.
Saraswati, the sacred stream,
In cosmic verses, where visions gleam.

In Rigveda's verses, Saraswati's song,
A river's tale, in scriptures long.
Upanishads whisper, in mystic tones,
Of Saraswati's flow, where wisdom owns.

In the Puranas' verses, Saraswati's trace,
A river's journey, in sacred space.
From the Himalayas to the Arabian Sea,
Saraswati's flow, a divine decree.

Jhelum, in the ancient realm,
A river's story, where history's helm.
Chenab's currents, in the cosmic tide,
A sacred stream, where cultures bide.

Ravi, the flow in the ancient breeze,
A river's journey, where history sees.
Sutlej's currents, in the fertile plain,
A sacred dance, in the riverine domain.

Brahmaputra, from the Himalayan height,
A river's saga, in the cosmic light.
Ganges and Yamuna, in sacred play,
A riverine journey, where virtues sway.

The Indus Valley, where history lies,
In the ancient realm, where civilizations rise.
Sapta Sindhu, the cradle of yore,
In the fertile valleys, where cultures explore.

In the Sat Yuga, the first age bright,
Sapta Sindhu, in pure light.
Vedic hymns echo, in sacred lands,
In the cosmic script, where time expands.

Treta Yuga unfolds, a grand design,
Ram's journey along the Sapta Sindhu line.
Ganges, Yamuna, in the epic tale,
In the riverine currents, where virtues prevail.

Dvapara Yuga, Krishna's cosmic play,
In Kurukshetra, where rivers lay.
Saraswati, the unseen flow,
In the ancient landscapes, where histories grow.

Kali Yuga's dawn, a shifting tide,
Sapta Sindhu, in time's stride.
Ganges' waters, in devotion's stream,
A sacred flow, in the cosmic dream.

So in Bharat's tapestry, where rivers flow,
Sapta Sindhu's currents, in history's glow.
From Vedas' hymns to timeless tales,
A riverine saga, where creation sails.

 Aadi

Ancient Bharat

In epochs old, where time began,
Ancient India, a mystic span.
From Himalayan peaks to southern shore,
Tales of yore, rich folklore.

Indus Valley's whispers in the dust,
Harappan secrets, artifacts robust.
Cities laid in geometric rhyme,
Civilization's bloom in ancient time.

Vedas chanted, hymns divine,
Knowledge sacred, like the sacred shrine.
Upanishads unravelling cosmic truth,
Sages seeking eternal youth.

Mahabharata's epic strife,
Kings and queens shaping life.
Arjuna's dilemma on Kurukshetra's plain,
Dharma's call, echoing refrain.

Buddha's serenity, under Bodhi's tree,
Noble Eightfold Path, set minds free.
Ashoka's edicts, pillars of peace,
Empires rose, their reigns would cease.

Silk routes bustling, trade's embrace,
Spices, gems, tales of grace.
Temples carved with intricate art,
Dravidian marvels, a cultural heart.

Through Gupta's golden age, a radiant beam,
Literature, science, a scholarly dream.
Ajanta's caves, art on rock,
A testament to time's tick-tock.

Ancient India, where gods did tread,
Shiva's dance, Vishnu's stead.
Yoga's wisdom, in the soul's chore,
A civilization's tale, forevermore.

 Aadi

Ramayana – Epic Tale of Sri Ram

In the sacred verses of ancient rhyme,
Ramayana breathes, transcending time.
Born in Valmiki's lyrical art,
A tale etched in every Bharatiya heart.

Valmiki's quill, a celestial stream,
Gave life to Rama, in a timeless dream.
Ayodhya's prince, in cradle's grace,
An epic's journey begins to trace.

Ramayana, an epic divine,
Rama's legacy, forever shine.
In the soul of Bharat, a sacred gleam,
A tale of dharma, in every theme.

Swayamvara's bow, a hero's might,
Rama wins Sita, love at first sight.
Vanvaas' exile, in the forest's embrace,
Challenges faced with unwavering grace.

Ramayana, an epic divine,
Rama's legacy, forever shine.
In the soul of Bharat, a sacred gleam,
A tale of dharma, in every theme.

Lanka's challenge, a demon's reign,
Hanuman's flight, across the main.
Sita's captive, in Ravana's hold,
A saga of courage, penance untold.

Kshatriya dharma, on Dharma's quest,
In the war of right, each warrior's best.
Rama's bow, a cosmic twine,
In Lanka's night, victory's sign.

Ayodhya's joy, a kingdom's delight,
Rama returns, ending the night.
Rama Rajya, a golden reign,
In every heart, the epic's gain.

In every heart, Ramayana's flame,
A timeless saga, forever the same.
Goswami Tulsidas' devotion profound,
In the verses of Ramcharitmanas, resound.

Ramayana, an epic divine,
Rama's legacy, forever shine.
In the soul of Bharat, a sacred gleam,
A tale of dharma, in every theme.

Aadi

Shubh Deepawali

In the heart of night, a festival bright,
Lights dance, a symphony of warm delight.
Lamps aglow, dispelling the dark,
A celebration, a radiant spark.

Diwali's here, a tale untold,
Of joy and love, in lanterns unfold.
Colours ablaze, in every street,
A tapestry of cultures, oh, so sweet.

Crackling fireworks paint the sky,
Whispers of happiness, soaring high.
Families gather, in warmth and grace,
A festival of lights, an embrace.

Candles flicker, in windows wide,
Symbolic flames, hope as our guide.
Through darkness, a path they create,
A festival that binds, love and fate.

 Aadi

An Ode to Hanuman Chalisa

In the heart of devotion, a hymn takes flight,
Hanuman Chalisa, in the cosmic light.
Goswami Tulsidas, with pen in hands,
Wove verses on Ganga's sacred banks.

Jai Hanuman, the mighty and wise,
A celestial hymn that eternally flies.
In Tulsidas' words, devotion flows,
A sacred river, where devotion grows.

"Yug Sahastra Yojan Par Bhanu,"
A cosmic measure, in verses strewn.
Thousands of yojanas, a journey untold,
To the sunlit orb, where warmth unfolds.

Hanuman Chalisa, in celestial glow,
Echoes through realms, both high and low.
A hymn that transcends both space and time,
In every devotee's heart, it does chime.

On Lanka's shores, a devotion profound,
Hanuman leapt, with love unbound.
In Ashoka Vatika, a captive's plight,
Hanuman brought Sita back to the light.

With the strength of mountains, a formidable force,
Hanuman's mace, a divine discourse.
Bhima's roar, in Hanuman's might,
A symphony of power, in celestial light.

To the Himalayas, in a swift descent,
For Sanjeevani, Hanuman was sent.
With the mountain in hand, a healing grace,
In every trial, devotion held its place.

Lanka's flames, a fiery tide,
Hanuman's tail, with flames tied.
Ravan's fortress, in fiery sway,
A divine saga in the night's array.

With the Lord's ring, in Hanuman's hand,
A symbol of trust in the Rama's command.
To Ayodhya's walls, the news he bore,
Of Sita's rescue from Lanka's shore.

On Ganga's banks, where devotion is rife,
Tulsidas penned the verses of life.
Hanuman Chalisa, a celestial song,
In every devotee's heart, it belongs.

 Aadi

Mahabharata – An Epic Tale of Bharatvarsh

In the cosmic loom of ages past,
Mahabharata's saga is cast.
An epic tale of honour and strife,
A timeless journey through mortal life.

Kuru's realm, a kingdom's birth,
In the soil of Bharat, an epic's worth.
Kings and queens in lineage trace,
Mahabharata begins its embrace.

A dice game's turn, a fateful night,
Pandavas' fortunes take a flight.
Exiled to the forest's green,
A twist in fate, a destined scene.

Amidst the Kurukshetra's vast plain,
Arjuna's turmoil, a warrior's bane.
Krishna's counsel, a celestial guide,
In the Bhagavad Gita, truths reside.

Mahabharata, a tapestry unfold,
Threads of dharma, in epics old.
Destiny's dance, a cosmic rhyme,
In every age, through endless time.

Bhishma's vow, a sacrifice sworn,
In Kurukshetra, war is born.
Kings and warriors, a cosmic clash,
On the battlefield, destinies crash.

Draupadi's plight, a woman's cry,
Karna's pathos, 'neath a fateful sky.
Injustice faced, honour torn,
Mahabharata's lessons born.

Yudhishthira's moral maze,
In Dharma's web, a king's phase.
In exile's dust and war's debris,
Mahabharata unfolds destiny.

Hastinapura, a kingdom's crest,
In the epic's heart, a city blessed.
Dynasties rise and dynasties fall,
Mahabharata narrates it all.

In every heart, Mahabharata's beat,
A cosmic rhythm, both bitter and sweet.
Through ages gone and ages to be,
The epic's echo, eternally free.

 Aadi

Krishna Consciousness

In the tapestry of time, a celestial melody,
Lord Krishna emerges, divinity's decree.
A cosmic avatar, in Bharat's embrace,
A sage, a statesman, a symbol of grace.

Krishna, Bharat's eternal son,
In every heart, his tale is spun.
Scientific truths in ancient lore,
A timeless essence, forevermore.

In Vrindavan's groves, a flute's sweet sound,
Echoes through ages, wisdom profound.
Krishna's melody, a cosmic dance,
In every heart, a divine trance.

In the battle of life, a charioteer wise,
Krishna guides Arjuna, truth in his eyes.
The Bhagavad Gita, a timeless song,
Guiding humanity, where they belong.

Dwaraka, a city by the ocean's side,
A kingdom flourished, in Krishna's stride.
A legacy of virtue, justice, and might,
Dharma's beacon, in the cosmic light.

To Bharat and beyond, his teachings soar,
Universal truths, an eternal core.
Love, duty, righteousness he imparts,
In every soul, Krishna's wisdom starts.

In Krishna's leela, a cosmic ballet,
Scientific rhythms, in time's array.
A dance of atoms, a celestial play,
In every particle, his presence lay.

A lover of nature, cows by his side,
Krishna in Gokul, nature as his guide.
A lesson profound in environmental care,
In Krishna's footsteps, humanity's prayer.

Yadnya's wheel, a cosmic flow,
Krishna's wisdom, a timeless show.
Sacrifice and service, in unity,
A cosmic law, in divinity.

The Sudarshan Chakra, a cosmic wheel,
In the fabric of time, its light does feel.
A symbol of justice, in cosmic flight,
Krishna's justice, eternal and bright.

In devotion's ocean, hearts immerse,
Krishna's love, a universe.
Bharat's gift to humanity's quest,
In Krishna's love, find eternal rest.

In Bharat's legacy, Krishna's name,
A timeless flame, in the cosmic frame.
Scientific and devotional, hand in hand,
Krishna's contribution, a cosmic strand.

In Kurukshetra's field, a cosmic stage,
The Bhagavad Gita, wisdom's sage.
Krishna speaks, in verses profound,
Eternal truths, the universe resound.

Paths of knowledge, devotion, and action,
Krishna's guidance, a cosmic transaction.
Yoga's essence, in verses revealed,
In every seeker's heart, the Gita sealed.

Duty and righteousness, Dharma's code,
In Gita's verses, a divine road.
Krishna unfolds life's purpose and plan,
A guide for every woman and man.

In detachment lies true liberation,
Krishna's lesson, a divine narration.
Perform your duties, with hearts surrendered,
Gita's teachings, eternally remembered.

Krishna reveals the cosmic form,
Unity in diversity, a divine norm.
In every being, his presence found,
A universal love, forever unbound.

Know the self, Krishna declares,
In Gita's verses, self-realization flares.
A lamp in the dark, wisdom's might,
Gita's essence, eternal light.

In the Gita's verses, Krishna's voice,
A timeless guide, humanity's choice.
Scientific and devotional, hand in hand,
Krishna's legacy, forever to withstand.

From Mathura's cradle to Dwarka's throne,
Krishna's legacy in every corner known.
A kingdom prosperous, grand, and divine,
In Dwarka's embrace, Krishna did shine.

To Puri's shores, a sacred tale,
Where Krishna's heart, a cosmic trail.
'Brahma padarth,' the eternal beat,
In Jagannath's temple, a sacred seat.

Jagannath Puri, where pilgrims unite,
In Krishna's grace, a sacred rite.
Unity in diversity, a cosmic plan,
In Puri's heart, Krishna's clan.

From Mathura's embrace to Dwarka's might,
In Jagannath's heart, Krishna's light.
Scientific and devotional, hand in hand,
Krishna unifies, a cosmic strand.

 Aadi

Gita – A Song Divine

In the hush of Kurukshetra's war-torn morn,
A celestial discourse, by Krishna, is born.
The Geeta unfolds, on the battlefield's stage,
A timeless scripture, a wisdom sage.

Arjuna stands, his spirit in strife,
'Midst kith and kin, pondering life.
A warrior's duty, a moral dilemma,
In the midst of kin, a troubled enigma.

Krishna, the charioteer, with a divine decree,
Unveils the truth, timeless and free.
The soul is eternal, beyond birth and death,
A cosmic journey, beyond mortal breath.

Gita, the song, on Kurukshetra's plain,
Wisdom profound, breaking every chain.
A cosmic melody, in verses divine,
Guiding the soul, through life's design.

Paths to liberation, a yogic array,
Karma, Bhakti, and Jnana's highway.
Duty-bound actions, devotion's embrace,
Knowledge profound, the soul to grace.

Life's fleeting moments, like a river's flow,
Impermanence whispers, in every echo.
A cosmic cycle, of birth and decay,
Krishna's wisdom, lighting the way.

In surrender's lap, find peace untold,
A sanctuary for the spirit to hold.
Devotion's flame, a sacred fire,
Guiding the soul, higher and higher.

Yoga's union, the seeker's quest,
In stillness and breath, find the crest.
Union with God, the ultimate goal,
The essence of Yoga, a harmonious soul.

On Kurukshetra's stage, in war's embrace,
The Geeta's wisdom, a timeless grace.
In every heart, its verses resound,
Eternal echoes, profound and unbound.

 Aadi

Historical Legends of Bharat

Adiyogi – The First Yogi

In the realm where Himalayan echoes ring,
A dance began, a celestial fling.
Adiyogi, the first yogi, arose,
In stillness and dance, his wisdom flows.

Over Fifteen thousand years ago, in the cosmic embrace,
Adiyogi danced, a mystic trace.
In stillness profound, he found his space,
An ecstatic dance, a divine grace.

The Himalayas witnessed this cosmic play,
As Shiva danced in the night and day.
His ecstasy, a celestial ballet,
A dance that led minds astray.

Adiyogi, the originator of yoga's seed,
In human minds, a sacred deed.
People intrigued, a mystery to read,
Adiyogi's dance, a spiritual creed.

People came, they waited, they left,
Except for seven, their hearts theft.
Determined to know, in their hearts cleft,
Adiyogi's wisdom, they deftly heft.

Day by day, week by week, they prepared,
Years passed, devotion bared.
Adiyogi's grace, for the ones who dared,
The seven, a saga shared.

On a full moon day, the solstice turned,
Adiyogi's gaze, the learners earned.
He transformed into the first Guru,
they discerned, On Guru Purnima, knowledge burned.

On Kanti Sarovar's banks, the transmission divine,
Adiyogi's knowledge, through space and time.
Seven sages shone, a luminous sign,
The Saptarishis, in wisdom's shrine.

Sent in directions, diverse they flew,
Yogic science, in cultures anew.
Strands of wisdom, colours they drew,
The Saptarishis, the cosmic crew.

Adiyogi's legacy, the seven unfold,
The yogic sciences, in tales retold.
A human's evolution, an ancient mould,
Beyond limitations, a truth foretold.

In the dance of existence, a human quest,
Adiyogi's wisdom, an eternal jest.
Evolve beyond, in the grand cosmic jest,
Adiyogi's call, a timeless bequest.

Aadi

Sapta Rishis – The seven Sages

In the twilight of eternity, where legends unfold,
Seven sages emerged, in a tale ancient and bold.
Adiyogi, the first yogi, bestows the gift divine,
Yoga's wisdom, a knowledge pure, to the Sapta Rishis entwined.

From the sacred hands of Shiva, they received the flame,
A cosmic gift, the essence of the eternal game.
Seven souls enlightened, with wisdom they'd share,
Sapta Rishis, bearers of knowledge rare.

Vashishta, the sage of cosmic harmony,
To the land of the rising sun, his legacy we see.
A cradle of civilization in the East,
Yoga's teachings, a timeless feast.

In the heart of southern India, Agastya set his gaze,
Spreading yoga's roots, in mystical ways.
A beacon of wisdom, across the gentry,
Ancient tales echo, in the Indian elementary.

In the Mesopotamian lands, Bhrigu's flame,
A river of knowledge, a historical claim.
Sumerians and Akkadians, in the Fertile Crescent's glow,
Yoga's whispers, in the archaeological show.

To the North, to the land of the Scythians bold,
Jamadagni's wisdom, like tales of old.
The steppes of Russia, where history begins,
Yoga's influence, in the ancient winds.

Atri, the sage, in the Western expanse,
To Europe's shores, in a mystical trance.
From the Druids to the ancient Celts,
Yoga's echoes, where the folklore tells.

To the East, to the islands of the rising sun,
Gautama's teachings, where Japan is spun.
Shaping civilizations with enlightened might,
Yoga's legacy, in the Japanese light.

Kashyapa, the sage, to the Kashmir valley ,
In the lands of the Pandits really.
Yoga's roots, in the Himalayan lore,
A cradle of civilization, a heaven for sure.

In the rhythmic dance of Sapta Rishis' tale,
Civilizations born, in a mystical trail.
Archaeological whispers, folklore's embrace,
Mankind owes its grace to the sages' base.

In the threads of time, where legends weave,
Sapta Rishis' wisdom, a gift to retrieve.
A debt of gratitude, to the cosmic seven,
For making us civilized, in the dance of heaven.

 Aadi

Lankapati Ravana

In Lanka's realm, where shadows dance,
Ravana rises, a complex trance.
A multi-headed rakshasa king,
In history's echo, his tales sing.

Born of Vishrava, the sage profound,
Kaikesi's son, his fate unbound.
Evil threads entwined with learning's grace,
Ravana, a paradox, in time's embrace.

A scholar vast in shastras' might,
The Vedas' wisdom, his guiding light.
Shiva Tandava Stotra, his hymn,
In the echoes, Ravana's soul swims.

Abductor of Sita, in Lanka's hold,
Ashoka Vatika, where tales unfold.
Rama, with vanara army's might,
To Lanka's shores, a celestial flight.

Sugriva's support, a bond so deep,
Invasion launched, as shadows creep.
Ravana, the foe, with Lanka's might,
A battle waged, in dharma's light.

Scientific echoes, a historical page,
In Ramayana's script, an ancient stage.
Vanquisher of evil, Rama's might,
Sita rescued from Lanka's night.

A revered devotee of Shiva's grace,
In paradox, Ravana finds his place.
Images in temples, Shiva's kin,
In devotion deep, his soul within.

Mahayana's whisper, Laṅkā's tale,
In Buddhist Jatakas, his echoes prevail.
Jain Ramayanas, another lore,
Ravana's story, evermore.

In some scriptures, a doorkeeper cursed,
Vishnu's realm, in shadows immersed.
Emotional currents, sacred and deep,
Ravana's saga, in history's keep.

 Aadi

Jai Shri Ram

In Ayodhya's embrace, a king so divine,
Shri Ram, noble heart, in epic design.
With arrows true and valour bold,
A saga of righteousness, forever told.

Born 'neath starry cosmic signs,
In the moonlit night, destiny entwines.
Ayodhya's prince, with a bow so grand,
Champion of dharma, in every land.

Sita's love, a bond unbroken,
Through trials dark, their spirits awoken.
Loyalty and courage, his royal decree,
In the heart of the forest, by the sacred tree.

Hanuman, devoted, with leaps so vast,
Witty , clever, epitome of strength, that never last.
Vanquisher of evil, with a just might,
Bajarangbali, the embodiment of Rama's cosmic light.

In verses sung and scriptures scrolled,
The legend of prince Ram is forever told.
Guiding souls on the righteous way,
Maryada Purshottam Shri Ram, eternal, in hearts shall stay.

 Aadi

Jai Bajrang Bali!

In the cosmic realm where mystics tread,
Bajarang Bali, Hanuman, is widely spread.
A deity of strength, both heart and might,
A celestial force, a beacon of light.

With muscles of steel and a heart so pure,
Hanuman, the devotee, we all adore.
Superhuman strength, a legend unfolds,
Yet, wisdom and wit, his story beholds.

Number one devotee of Lord Ram,
In the epic tale, a loyal dram.
Across the yugas, his presence endures,
A cosmic dance, where divinity lures.

Through the ages, in devotion he thrives,
Across the yugas, where time derives.
Knowledgeable and clever, a celestial guide,
In Hanuman's embrace, devotees confide.

In the mystic echoes of Hanuman Chalisa,
A powerful hymn, a divine visa.
For devotees to connect, hearts unfurl,
In the chants, where devotion swirls.

Bajarang Bali, in every hue,
A mystical presence, both old and new.
Kind and clever, his virtues combine,
In the cosmic tapestry, forever to shine.

Oh, Hanuman, in devotion we sing,
To the devotee of Rama, let our hearts cling.
In the cosmic dance, where divinity calls,
Bajarang Bali, within every soul enthrals.

 Aadi

Pandit Vishnu Sharma – Shaper of Generations

In the ancient realm where wisdom flows,
Pandit Vishnu Sharma, knowledge he bestows.
With quill in hand, a sage of lore,
Crafting tales that endure evermore.

In Indian soil, where culture thrives,
Panchatantra's birth, where tales arrive.
Vishnu Sharma, a wordsmith wise,
Wove fables that time defies.

Five books unfold, a wisdom array,
In animal realms, the characters play.
The cunning jackal, the wise old crow,
Lessons in their tales to bestow.

Panchatantra's legacy, a timeless treasure,
Wisdom woven in tales, a cultural measure.
For generations, its tales unfurled,
Shaping minds in an ancient world.

In the court of king and commoner,
Panchatantra whispered, a sagely mentor.
Political wit, strategies bright,
A guide for rulers, day and night.

As languages changed, and empires grew,
Panchatantra's tales, to cultures it flew.
From Sanskrit's cradle, it spread its wings,
A cultural tapestry it forever brings.

Through wit and humour, life's truths revealed,
Morals in fable's guise, in hearts sealed.
Pandit Vishnu Sharma, a storyteller sage,
Left an indelible mark on history's page.

In the tapestry of tales, woven fine,
Vishnu Sharma's legacy, a timeless sign.
Panchatantra's gift to hearts that ponder,
A sage's echo, in wisdom's yonder.

 Aadi

Kalidasa

In the court of ancient times, a poet did reside,
Kalidasa, his name, with talents worldwide.
With words as his paintbrush, emotions he'd confide,
In the verses he wove, a world's beauty he'd describe.

In "Shakuntala," a love story's bloom,
He painted passion, in every room.
With nature's backdrop, a love's perfume,
Kalidasa's verses, an eternal heirloom.

From "Ritusamhara" to "Meghaduta's" flight,
Kalidasa's poetry, a celestial light.
In the grand tapestry of words, so bright,
He wove tales of love, in the day and the night.

In nature's beauty, his verses found birth,
Describing the Earth, in its infinite girth.
Kalidasa, a poet of immeasurable worth,
In the world of literature, a gem of great mirth.

So, let us honour this poet of yore,
Whose verses still enchant, as in days of yore.
Kalidasa's words, forever they'll pour,
In the hearts of those who seek and explore.

 Aadi

Aryabhatta – Beautiful Mind from Ancient Time

In ancient India's scholarly past,
A genius's legacy forever will last.
Aryabhatta, his knowledge so vast,
In the realms of mathematics, he cast.

He looked to the stars in the night's expanse,
And from their movements, he took a chance.
The number zero, a brilliant advance,
Aryabhatta's genius, a cosmic dance.

His work on pi, a mathematical key,
Unlocking circles' mysteries, you see.
In astronomy, he helped us to be,
Better observers of the celestial sea.

In history's pages, his name we find,
Aryabhatta, a brilliant, inquisitive mind.
In the annals of knowledge, he's enshrined,
In the cosmos of wisdom, forever aligned.

Aadi

Samrat Prithviraj Chauhan – Lion of Bharat

In the annals of time, where history unfurls,
A name echoes loud – Prithviraj Chauhan, a hero of swirls.
Amidst the dust of battles, his valour did gleam,
A sovereign's heart, like a warrior's dream.

Rajputana's lion, with a kingdom to defend,
Prithviraj Chauhan, on destiny's bend.
With steely gaze and an unwavering might,
He rode into the fray, where shadows take flight.

In the battlefield's theatre, a tale took shape,
Prithviraj's courage, an indomitable cape.
Sword in hand, and armour clad in gold,
A saga of valour, centuries have told.

Yet, in the grandeur, a bittersweet theme,
For love and loss wove through his esteemed.
Samyukta's name, a melody in his heart,
A love that endured, though worlds apart.

In the echoing canyons of history's domain,
Prithviraj Chauhan, a sovereign in the rain.
Through triumph and tragedy, his legend endures,
A timeless hymn, where bravery ensures.

Oh, Prithviraj, in the tapestry of time,
Your name etched in verses, a rhythm sublime.
A Rajput king, on history's grand stage,
In the echoes of valour, you forever engage.

 Aadi

Comprehending Comprehensions

Earthen Lamp – The Light Within

In the quiet of the darkest night,
An earthen lamp casts a gentle light.
A vessel of clay, so simple and plain,
Yet within it, a world of warmth to gain.

With a flicker and a soft, steady glow,
It banishes shadows, casting a magical show.
In its humble form, a radiant flow,
The earthen lamp, a beauty to bestow.

In Diwali's grace or a sacred shrine,
It spreads its light, a love divine.
A symbol of hope, in the design,
The earthen lamp, a treasure so fine.

It's flame dances with a graceful flair,
Whispering secrets in the midnight air.
In its luminous embrace, we find solace there,
The earthen lamp, a symbol so rare.

So, let us cherish this beacon of grace,
In its humble glow, our hearts we place.
An earthen lamp, in its gentle pace,
Fills our world with light's warm embrace.

 Aadi

Father – Son bond

In the circle of life, where moments are spun,
A father and son, two becoming one.
Through laughter and tears, they navigate life,
A bond so profound, amid joy and strife.

From the first steps taken, hand in hand,
To teaching life's lessons, helping understand.
A father imparts his wisdom and care,
A son learns and grows, a precious pair.

In the backyard, a game of catch they play,
Or sitting together, at the end of the day.
Shared dreams, shared hopes, hearts intertwined,
A bond of love, forever designed.

Through trials and triumphs, they stand as a team,
In the warmth of their love, it feels like a dream.
A father's strength, a son's guiding star,
Together they journey, no matter how far.

In the dance of life, where emotions reside,
A father and son, an eternal tide.
Not a scold, not a beat, just love's sweet song,
An embodiment of love, a bond so strong.

In the wrestling ring, where courage takes form,
Unbeaten, a wrestler, a brewing storm.
Olympic dreams, a path he once tread,
Family's call, he turned, love instead.

Shiva's essence, vibrant in his stride,
Energetic, pure, in life's turning tide.
A vision grand, a supreme athlete's grace,
Lost in service, a selfless embrace.

Life's teachings, whispered in deeds,
not words, Situational awareness, a song of the birds.
Courage, a beacon, an epitome true,
In his vibrant footsteps, I grew.

Empathy flowed in his every vein,
Others' joy over self's pain.
A visionary's mind, thoughts far and wide,
In his energetic aura, I'd confide.

In the ring and beyond, a hero he'd be,
Ready to help, a spirit so free.
Though gone, not absent, forever near,
In his everlasting intensity, I revere.

In the passage of time, as seasons roll on,
The father and son, their legacy drawn.
A connection unbroken, a love that won't cease,
In this timeless bond, they both find peace.

A father's legacy, a timeless art,
Carved in love, on the soul's own chart.
Emotions linger, in the heart's vast sea,
He lives on, an eternal part of me.

Aadi

Maa

In the tapestry of my life, a guiding light,
A beacon of love, in every step, so bright.
Maa, my mother, a being so sweet,
In her embrace, my world finds complete.

Her hands, like cradles, tender and warm,
Navigating life's storms, shielding from harm.
In the quiet moments, and laughter so free,
Maa, my mother, a melody to me.

With a heart that echoes compassion and care,
Her love's an anthem, in the open air.
In the canvas of memories, she paints with grace,
Maa, my mother, a timeless embrace.

Through seasons of joy and trials so tough,
Her resilience, a testament, strong enough.
In her eyes, a universe of stories untold,
Maa, my mother, a treasure to hold.

Her wisdom, a compass, in life's vast sea,
Guiding my sails, where I'm meant to be.
In the warmth of her love, a refuge I find,
Maa, my mother, the dearest of kind.

With every sunrise, and each twilight's glow,
Her love, an eternal river's gentle flow.
In the chapters of life, she's my constant theme,
Maa, my mother, the hero of my dream.

 Aadi

My BlunderBuss Grandmother

In the heart of our clan, a force of delight,
Our blunderbuss grandma, with all her might.
With silver hair and a whimsical grin,
A beacon of empowered woman, a lively human without a brim.

In the kitchen, she reigns like a culinary wizard,
Creating dishes that leave us quite bewildered.
Her recipes, a mystery of spice and sass,
Grandma's cooking: a culinary class.

With a shopping list as long as a winding road,
She ventures out, carrying a comical load.
Grocery bags swinging, a sight to see,
Our respected grandma, a shopping spree.

Her knitting needles click like a metronome,
A symphony of stitches, a crafty tome.
Scarves and sweaters, each with a twist,
Grandma's creations, hard to resist.

In her tales, the details may slightly stray,
A blunder here, a misstep there, they say.
Yet, we listen with love, eyes all aglow,
For grandma's stories steal the show.

Her sheer existence, a legendary feat,
A rollercoaster ride on every street.
With a lead foot and a fearless demeanour,
Our beloved grandma, a driving queen.

In the garden, she sows with whimsical grace,
Planting veggies in a chaotic embrace.
Tomatoes next to tulips, carrots with flair,
Grandma's garden, beyond compare.

So here's to our blunderbuss grandma so dear,
With laughter and love, she fills the air.
A respected matriarch, a source of cheer,
In her delightful blunders, we hold her near.

Aadi

Father's Demise

In the hush of night, a shadow fell,
A father, a legend, in life, he dwelled.
A wrestler's strength, a heart so bold,
An honest policeman, in stories told.

His laughter echoed, like a victorious cheer,
In the wrestling ring, his presence clear.
A superhuman, my hero true,
In every tale, his virtues grew.

All about love and devotion's art,
A father's essence, a beating heart.
Radiating love in every stride,
His nurturing energy, a comforting guide.

Leader by example, he paved the way,
In the light of love, he'd always stay.
Empathy flowed in every word,
Like a song of love, always heard.

Tears may flow like a river's tide,
But in our hearts, he'll forever reside.
In the stars, his spirit will forever shine,
A guiding light, a love divine.

Like Lord Rudra, his presence divine,
A cosmic dance in every storyline.
Brain function, a marvel to behold,
In the labyrinth of thoughts, stories unfold.

Hardworking beyond compare,
A dedication that filled the air.
A Shiva in our midst, we declare,
In his memory, we deeply care.

Though he's gone, his love remains,
In every heartbeat, in joys and pains.
For a father's love, so pure and true,
Lives on in us, in all that we do.

 Aadi

A Teenager's Plight!

In the tender years of youth, a spirit bold,
A teenager's dreams, a tale yet untold.
Yearning to carve a path, noble and true,
Against a tide of shadows, he endeavours to break through.

In the labyrinth of society, where shadows breed,
He faces the unwise, the negative seed.
A battlefield of ideals, where ignorance may reign,
Yet, he stands resolute, in the face of disdain.

For family, country, and society's plight,
He yearns to mend, to bring forth the light.
But entrenched are structures, with shadows cast,
A struggle unfolds, the die is cast.

Amidst the battle, a darker plot unfolds,
Black magic's tendrils, a story untold.
A malicious dance, on his family it preys,
Devouring precious years, in its wicked maze.

Yet, in the depth of adversity, he finds his might,
A warrior against the unwise, a beacon in the night.
Fighting not just the visible, but the unseen,
In the tapestry of challenges, a resilient sheen.

His dreams, a phoenix rising from the ash,
Against the currents, he fights the gnashing clash.
For family, country, and society's call,
He stands unwavering, breaking the darkened thrall.

In the crucible of struggle, his character refined,
A tapestry woven with threads intertwined.
For the teenager who battles, resilient and brave,
May his spirit triumph, the family & nation to save.

 Aadi

Brother in Arms

In the tapestry of life, a thread so dear,
A brother's love, so crystal clear.
My younger kin, my heart's stronghold,
In your innocence, a story unfolds.

A moral compass in this vast sea,
Guiding me to who I'm meant to be.
Your purity, a beacon so bright,
In your gaze, I find my guiding light.

A critic for my wellbeing, sincere,
A voice of reason, calm and clear.
Through life's maze, you walk by my side,
A bond unbroken, where love resides.

Responsibilities, burden on your youth,
A testament to your unwavering truth.
You've shouldered more than your tender years,
Yet, in your eyes, no trace of fears.

Stand tall, dear brother, in love we confide,
You, my ally, forever by my side.
The weight you carry, heavy and grand,
Yet, together, we'll weather this shifting sand.

Your health, a treasure, we yearn to restore,
To see you flourish, strong once more.
In your essence, the purest joy,
My little brother, forever my buoy.

In the symphony of life, our notes entwine,
A brother's love, an eternal sign.
Through highs and lows, thick and thin,
In your love, a lifetime we begin.

Aadi

A Broken Doll

In the attic's dusty embrace, a broken doll weeps,
Fractured porcelain dreams, where sorrow slowly seeps.
Once adorned in silk, a cherished confidante,
Now a silent witness to a tragic, loveless dance.

Eyes that once sparkled, now glazed with despair,
Cracks on porcelain skin, whispers of a love affair.
Torn lace and shattered limbs, a puppet's tragic fate,
In the corner of solitude, abandoned by time and date.

Once cradled in warmth, a treasured childhood friend,
Now abandoned, discarded, a tale of a heart's bitter end.
A symphony of silence echoes through the hollow chest,
A broken doll's lament, a tale of love unexpressed.

Threads of memories unravel, a tapestry undone,
In the realm of forgotten toys, where shadows overrun.
Yet, in the brokenness, a beauty still resides,
A poignant reminder of love's fleeting tides.

 Aadi

Plight Of Farmers

Beneath the sun's relentless gaze, in fields of toil,
A farmer's plight, a tale of endless soil.
Hands calloused, worn by the weight of the earth,
Sowing dreams in furrows, of abundant worth.

Seasons dance in a rhythmic, fickle waltz,
A farmer's heart bears the burden it exhales.
Raindrops, a prayer, on parched, cracked lands,
Fingers entwined with hope, in nature's hands.

The plough cuts through the canvas of the dawn,
Yet, in the struggle, dreams are reborn.
Seeds of hope in each calloused palm,
A farmer's resilience, a quiet psalm.

Debts as heavy as the summer air,
Yet, they sow their hopes without despair.
Crops, like children, they tenderly rear,
In the cycle of seasons, a silent tear.

From sunrise's blush to twilight's embrace,
A farmer's journey, a relentless chase.
In the amber waves, stories untold,
Of harvests reaped and dreams unfold.

Oh, the farmer, guardian of the earth,
In the furrows of struggle, they find their worth.
A stoic figure against the setting sun,
A tale of resilience, forever spun.

 Aadi

ICC World Cup 2023 – We Stand With Team India

In the cricket arena, where battles unfold,
A salute to Team India, fearless and bold.
In the World Cup final, where dreams take flight,
"Well played, Team India," in our hearts tonight.

A closely-knit unit, a spirit untamed,
In the face of defeat, their resilience is named.
Despite the loss, their journey profound,
In unity, Team India, forever renowned.

Yet, a reflection on the path we tread,
In our celebration, where is the team's thread?
Individual heroism, a spotlight so bright,
But team spirit's glory, our true guiding light.

As records tumble, and hype takes flight,
In the team's success, let's find our delight.
For in each player, a part of the whole,
A symphony of talents, a united soul.

Glenn Maxwell's innings, a turning tide,
A lesson for India in cricket's wide ride.
Australia emerged, a fighting crew,
Team spirit ignited, a lesson anew.

Mohammad Shami, a warrior's heart,
In his fight, a tale to impart.
Bumrah and Siraj, the bowling grace,
In the cricketing realm, they find their place.

Rohit Sharma, a fearless guide,
A mindset new, in cricket's stride.
Dominating, fearless, a mindset earned,
A lesson for a nation, where wisdom's discerned.

In this tough time, we stand by the team,
Through the loss, and in the dream.
But let's evolve as a nation, wise and true,
In celebrating wins, and losses too.

Honest, transparent, respectful, we strive,
Vulnerability-based trust, where talents thrive.
In conquering fear, we find our might,
Encouraging healthy conflicts, in wisdom's light.

Ask the right questions, speak truthfully clear,
A nation evolving, with courage near.
Strike the balance in how we treat our pride,
In victory's joy, and in loss's stride.

Let's not praise too much, nor let them fall,
In Team India's journey, find balance in all.
For commitment, accountability, results in hand,
In this cricketing tale, let our nation stand.

 Aadi

Digital India Stack

In the digital age, where progress aligns,
India Stack emerges, where innovation shines.
A unified platform, with layers distinct,
Solving hard problems, in the digital instinct.

First comes Presenceless, controversial yet grand,
Biometrics stored, a unique digital stand.
Aadhaar's fingerprints, a citizen's key,
In the digital realm, where identity is free.

Paperless Layer follows, records linked online,
Personal data associated, in the digital sign.
eKYC's rapid verification, a paperless chase,
In the digital landscape, where records embrace.

Cashless Layer, a single interface grand,
National banks and wallets, in one digital strand.
Unified Payments Interface, a cashless route,
In the digital realm, where payments sprout.

Consent Layer, where control lies,
Security maintained, where data flies.
Privacy's guardian, in the digital quest,
In the layers of India Stack, where innovation rests.

Aadhaar's journey in 2009, a starting spark,
Universal ID numbers, in the digital arc.
Biometrics and time, authentication expands,
In the digital landscape, where access demands.

e-KYC follows, in electronic Know Your Customer's sway,
Paperless verification, in the digital relay.
eSign emerges, electronic signature's grace,
In the digital realm, where legality takes place.

Unified Payments Interface, a cashless bloom,
Digital transactions, in the digital room.
DigiLocker unfolds, documents' digital stream,
In the digital space, where certificates gleam.

Demonetization in 2016, a turning tide,
₹500 and ₹1,000 notes, in cashless stride.
Forgeries and money-laundering, the official cause,
In the digital realm, where currency withdraws.

Challenges arise, privacy's call,
Supreme Court's ruling, as rights enthral.
A fundamental right, privacy's decree,
In the digital landscape, where rights agree.

Ernst & Young acclaim, a global benchmark set,
India Stack's prowess, a worldwide bet.
A pilot with Capital Float, a fintech delight,
In the digital journey, where loans take flight.

Presenceless, paperless, cashless, and consent,
India Stack's layers, in innovation's event.
A digital revolution, where progress aligns,
In the layers of India Stack, where the future shines.

 Aadi

Acknowledgement

In the symphony of life, where eternal reverberations find their tune, my heart overflows with thanks to those who have been the notes and melodies in my journey.

To Isha Foundation and Sadhguru Shri Jaggi Vasudev, whose profound teachings and transformative practices have illuminated my path, guiding me towards self-discovery and inner well-being. Your wisdom has been the North Star in the tapestry of my existence.

To the Hyderabad Runners Society, where the rhythm of my footsteps merged with the collective heartbeat of a running community. The miles we traversed together, the shared victories, and the unspoken camaraderie shaped not just my fitness but my spirit.

To all the individuals, experiences, and moments that I encountered in this beautiful journey—each a brushstroke in the painting of my life. To the ones who challenged me, the ones who supported me, and the ones who simply passed through, leaving an indelible mark.

To my family—the pillars of my strength and the keepers of my roots. To my father, whose love and teachings continue to guide me, even in his physical absence. To my mother, whose nurturing embrace is my sanctuary. To my younger brother, Avani, a beacon of innocence and purity. To my sisters, Moksha and Kshama, whose names embody the essence of liberation and forgiveness.

A special acknowledgment to the blessings of my ancestors and forefathers, whose unseen hands have shaped the trajectory of my life. Though not present in the physical realm, their influence and guidance are palpable in every step I take.

This book, 'Eternal Reverberations,' is not just mine; it belongs to the intricate dance of connections and influences that have coloured my world. Thank you all for being a part of this symphony.

About The Author

Aditya is A Fusion of Tech Mastery, Fitness Passion, Yogic energy, Mythological Insight, Love for History, and Artistic Talent. A seasoned tech product enthusiast, tech influencer, ultra marathoner, yoga practitioner, mythologist, author, an ardent traveller and a history buff with over a decade in software product management. A versatile leader, Aditya has crafted and scaled innovative B2B products, showcasing a unique blend of tech prowess, leadership, and a rich tapestry of interests.

Meet Aditya:

Holistic Lifestyle: An avid ultra marathon runner, yoga practitioner, and fitness influencer, Aditya is committed to physical, mental and spiritual well-being for the greater good.

Mythological Lens: Aditya intertwines mythologies with modern tech and sciences, offering a unique perspective on the ancient and contemporary.

History Enthusiast: With a love for history, Aditya explores culturally rich sites globally, connecting the dots between mythology, history, science and technology deriving a distinguished perspective on WHY, HOW and What part of the equation for human civilization.

Artistic Flair: Aditya showcases his artistic talent through captivating landscapes and performing vocals of Sanskrit chants , adding a creative touch to his diverse skill set.

Sportsman: Proficient in lawn tennis, chess, and cricket, Aditya's love for sports mirrors his strategic thinking and competitive spirit.

Product Maestro: Aditya navigates the entire product lifecycle, launching high-ROI products and leading top-performing teams.

Community Contributor: Beyond the corporate realm, Aditya is an active contributor to society. His involvement with the Isha Foundation of Sadhguru Jaggi Vasudeva and the Hyderabad Runners Society reflects his commitment to giving back. Aditya also shares his wealth of knowledge by occasionally writing and speaking on various topics related to product management & technical innovations, Ancient Indian history and wisdom, running and holistic wellbeing at various industry-recognized platforms.

Leadership Excellence: A natural collaborator, Aditya builds and mentors top-tier engineering teams, showcasing organizational and management finesse.

Authorship Journey: As Aditya delves into authorship, his book promises a rich tapestry of science, fitness, mythology, history, patriotism and artistic expression, offering readers a holistic experience.

Linkedin.com/in/adityapandeyadi

Facebook.com/Aditya.pandey.31105

x.com/Pandey_Aadityaa

Instagram.com/adityaveshpandey

www.ingramcontent.com/pod-product-compliance
Lightning Source LLC
LaVergne TN
LVHW010606160826
845677LV00013B/3282

* 9 7 9 8 8 9 2 3 3 7 4 7 2 *